QUIDDITIES
Poems New & Selected

Quiddities

Poems New & Selected

JOSEPH BRADDOCK

HARRY CHAMBERS/PETERLOO POETS

First published in 1985
by Harry Chambers/Peterloo Poets
Treovis Farm Cottage, Upton Cross, Liskeard, Cornwall PL14 5BQ

© 1985 by Joseph Braddock

All rights reserved. No part of this publication may be reproduced, stored in a retrieval system, or transmitted, in any form or by any means, electronic, mechanical, photocopying, recording, or otherwise without the prior permission of the publisher.

ISBN 0 905291 72 7

Printed in Great Britain by
Latimer Trend & Company Ltd, Plymouth

ACKNOWLEDGEMENTS are due to the editors of the following journals and anthologies in whose pages some of the newer poems in the present collection first appeared: *Contemporary Review, Life And Letters, New Poetry 3* (Art Council, 1977), *P. E. N. Broadsheet, Poetry Review, Poetry South East 1*.

The two poems marked † in the Contents list first appeared in *Sark & Other Poems* (Basil Blackwell, 1930).

The poem marked ⊕ in the Contents list first appeared in *The Pilgrim Shadow* (Duckworth, 1928).

The 16 poems marked * in the Contents list first appeared in *No Stronger Than A Flower. Poems 1935–1960* (Hale, 1960).

Cover illustration: Mansell Collection.

To my Wife

Contents

	page
*Modes of Feeling	9
Moving Into Aquarius	13
*These Images	14
*The Choice	15
†Sea-Birds on The Scillies	16
*Art Examination	18
*Van Gogh	19
*The Crusaders Entering Constantinople In 1204	20
*Black Cat In Prunus Tree	21
⊕ La Cathédrale Engloutie	22
Fifty Summers Back	23
*The House Of Certainty	24
*In Memoriam: Sidney Keyes	25
*Poem for Winter	26
*Saul At Endor	28
*How Far Those Days of Peace Seem Now	29
Life	30
*Lazarus	31
*Poem for Autumn	32
†Butterflies, Moths	35
*The Butterfly	38
Oleander	39
Greek Folk Song	40
The Theophilos Museum, Mytilene	41
From Ormos Grikou, Patmos	42
From Taormina Once	43
Abroad	44
Each Quiddity	45
To Candida Born	46
Comfort	47
In Time of Tribulation	48
Two Silences	51
Be Still Then ...	52
Evensong	53

Modes Of Feeling

(To Paul Roche)

I

The girl with the mussed hair
Moves about the kitchen in the morning magic
That gilds the glossy tea-leaves in the tray
The wax chunk of soap, saucepan lids
And metal wool of the scourer.

Magic persists, light percolates
To butter cold and paper-wrapped
Brown eggs, breadcrust, full milk bottles
With buff top layers of cream.
The brick floor thrills the girl's bare feet,
Who opens the door to the cat.

She stands to watch the sun come up,
The morning cyclorama of the ridge
White oast-cowls lit, two pigeons!
Her silk wrap falls apart, freeing
Her life-demanding breasts.

She humours the muscular miniature puma perched on the
    canteen
Voice sounding, cross-patch for his breakfast.
There is dew on his whiskers.
His eyes, blue arabesque, absorb her scrutiny.
She sees with wonder how the conquering sun
Shows through an ear a network of red veins
A hairy ear outlined in mapping ink
With a red branching vein down the middle.

II

The boy by the seashore dreams of far lands.
He looks at rocks, stones, tar, black strong-smelling weed;
Hears cries, sees the fuss and slow flap of fair gulls.
There is a bird stuck in the blue air, a pale marble!
Shadows of gulls crossing the macintosh shine of wet sand,
White and black spots of gulls and jackdaws marking the rusted
  chalk of the cliff face.
That was a young one that gave a loud squawk.

But what lies over the wide wealth of water
Siren-blue flashing water
In-crinkling, foam-pushing waves?
What lies over the water for me?
He dreams, as he has dreamed before, of great tasks
His courage will make seem light
Of obstacles to match his strength.
He longs to grow up.

Already he has found in the shapes of stones
The female form, shining and supple
As when Aphrodite came to man out of the sea
Breast, flank and buttock, passive to man's positive
And wondered what it may be to love a woman.

So he must dream of love and adventure
His eyes not seeing years pile up on the worn spinach breakwater
While a growing tide moves in his blood.

III

The tear in the old man's eye
At the day's end is for what did not happen.
Inert, half listening to evening birds
Also hearing the grind of Time
He leans forward dejected in his deck-chair
Hands pressed between bony knees

Bearing his neck's wastage with hard-won wisdom
The enveloping pressure, the grip of manacles.
The tear in the old man's eye
Is for the false prelude, the insulting shortness.

Time's vicious fingers bring mind to the surface
Dry fingers clutch his vulnerable bald head.
He feels the skeleton beneath flesh
Holes behind anguished eyes
Harks the mocking cuckoo, smells soft lilac
Knows he had thought too little of the sundial.

I am a winter fly whose strength must hourly ebb
My hands move feeble as a dying crab's claws
These swollen veins are perished rubber
Hair left will grow on in the grave.

All's past, lost, broken but one thing beauty:
The cry of the yellowhammer, evening bells
That long-tailed static trembling kestrel
Sunlight thick shafted down from thundercloud
Throwing gold scarves to catch in oak and ash.

These yield delight still to my inward eye.
Such will I hold in my thought.

IV

But the poet who walks alone
Knows that the girl's ecstasy
The boy's expectancy, the old man's melancholy
Are each a vagrant valuable moment
A brief—yet long—particular image starring
And defying the centuries
Transcending time and place.

Look in the snug of an inn, under that dark table
A poodle's head, a black dahlia, glistening eyes.
Any dog grasping a bone, why he's been there
Since Chaucer took the road to Canterbury
Or Odysseus went home to Ithaca.
That sleek cat, see, sharpening sadist claws
For the voracious shrew's
Protracted terror, is as durable
As glazed Egyptian porcelain from tombs.

Manifold incarnations, inbeings
In an ascending cycle
Point to the warm touch of a human hand.
That bird you hear whistling his heart out
Forlornly went unheeded,
While scythe-winged swifts tore shrieking through the sky,
Swift dropped on swift in high pure heaven to mate
Unmarked of man. Flowers breathed their fragrances
Aeons before brutes lurked to smell them.

All forms of life, each separate quiddity
Shadow the divine perfect
Stirring the conscious soul
Bound to race memories,
Speak equally through a cell or Saturn's rings.
Ahead peaks gleam, waves glow:
Salt odour of the glowing wave to those long parched by land
Presage a Sea no mortal mind may sail.

Moving Into Aquarius

Some say we're 'moving into Aquarius'
New planetary epoch this.
Think then of lost civilizations
After the first kiss

With winter and summer changing
Fir-paws of loaded snow,
The rattle in the seed-pod
The soil where seed will go.

Creator makes all creatures
From dense to fragile live.
Yet mountain, sea and wildflower
Must all prove fugitive.

God-white, God's light
Rising across the land
A seamless love enwoven
For men to understand.

A one-ness, a compassion,
Archaic the creed of war
When man, the master now of peace
Has colonized a star.

These Images

These images were mortal without love
Pithless, unfocussed, would lie down to die:
The bracing rain driving towards the shore,
The shags' sea race; then on the lower cliff
Campion, montbretia, ragwort, tufted crests
Of knapweed and the corraline
Delicate tamarisk, pagoda-bells
Warm fuchsia sways for colour, all the pomp
Purple and gold of August's panoply.
These images were empty less your love.
Love is a lamp within the alabaster,
Irradiation in the bowl of sky
That stirs my life to wonder, blazons earth.
Love is the soundless flight of a white bird
Which else were flesh and feathers and no more.

The Choice

There is no poetry unless we make it
Not to stand out upon the neutral page
Only, but formed in our warm hearts as well;
Unless we spin it from our psychic entrails
As the spider her delicate web ashine with dew
Which catches not mere food for body
But traps all lights and stars, the company of Heaven.
Vain runs the spring tide in the estuary
The way the small waves hurry and stumble on;
O vain the red legs poking in the flats
Hunched head of oyster-catcher which boatmen call
The sea-pie for his clear pipe can be mute,
Beauty is nothing to dead ears and eyes,
O may I wake and tremble, stand alive!
The curlew cries, deluded, to deaf ears.

Sea-Birds on The Scillies

Where the porpoise turns a lazy fin
And the seal slips off the lonely rock
Weird pillar granite stands the shock
Of dead-white surges labouring in.
The streamline sea-birds come and go
About the archipelago.

Terns flash curved wings, sea-swallow white
Hang like bunched lace, drop, slap the foam
Rebound at once; then oar back home
To a small bare rock their nesting-site
Long fish in beak, pass to and fro
Fays of the archipelago.

Each nesting bird has his prized fort
As snake-necked cormorant, lesser shag,
On inaccessible much fouled crag
Will guard the blue eggs of their sort:
So razorbill and guillemot
Breed in the archipelago.

Marble by pearl of herring gull
Gannets declare their passage far
Following shoals. On Annet are
Beneath sea-pinks, deep burrows full
Of shearwaters that nightly go
Swift on the archipelago,

Though many die under the beak
Of 'black-backs', vultures of the sea.
That clown sea-parrot pleases me
The puffin like a painted freak
Who eyes me till I let him go
To skim the archipelago.

But I exult most in the wild
Sorrowful call of the ringed plover;
With oyster catchers piping over
And brown rock pipits tinkling mild,
Mingling with ocean's drag and flow
Over the archipelago.

Today I hear the cuckoo chime
His double note beyond the tide.
Why comes he here? As I abide
Fortuitous, and make this rhyme?
He rings his bell that all may know
He's crossed the archipelago.

Art Examination

In your red and white small check American blouse
Blue faded jeans rolled halfway to your knees
And floor-soiled naked feet, with burnished hair
Fringed, mussed, and tied in a pony-tail you are
God's loveliest imagination.
Child, as I watch you work your brown face shows
Unclouded, clear of thwarting. No sour memories
Of baffled vision, hopes crushed; but flushed with these
Creative thoughts you put them quick into action
Designing your own pattern to the gayest fraction.
So deeply I am moved knowing the years will take you
To trouble you some evil way, to spoil or make you.

Van Gogh

Your turbulent intensity
Painted the poor with truth and pity:
Age-old griefs, the prisoners' slouching round
The near starving, the lonely wife and love's ripe zones
But also bony knees, drooped anguished dugs.
You painted too new ploughed ripe purple fields
The shining airy grace May orchard yields
Candescent blossom dancing to greet sweet cloud
Prancing branches on patched yellow ground.

In Vincent's room you proved how matter lives
With barely static bed, floor, table, chairs.
At night in Arles your stars were Catherine-wheels
The café figures warmed in southern trance.

The Sun both angel and devil was
A murderous mirror but vision's glass.
Sunflowers have eyes, jagged hair of flame
Cornfields are gold that has yet no name
Where the quivering lark goes, cypress upward flows.

When from dire storm wrack a flock of crows
Swept blackly down on the yellow wheat
You shot yourself. Death's stroke was feat.
A giver of beauty you stand afar
It takes Death to reach a star.

The Crusaders Entering Constantinople In 1204

(Eugene Delacroix)

Massed in fuliginous cloud Christ's bannered men
Storm in the old world's burning capital
Bewildered. Destruction devours itself
As blood, voluptuousness and death ripen:
The bare grooved back, black waterfall of hair
Bow, cringe from the flesh-piercing spear.
Behind, a bloody Bosphorus, fruit of despair.

O Delacroix, dark tiger! Valiant painter!
The solitary largeness of your art
Accuses our plight. At brooding intervals
You felt the energy of a shifting world
Poised on a hair-bridge across disaster;
Chopin's music 'like a bird of brilliant plumage
Fluttering over the abyss', admired with heart and mind.

Pity our cuckoo-palace of blue air
Poisoned by a mushroom cloud of fear.

Black Cat In Prunus Tree

Dark demon angel by royal right
Sits Satan in a world of light
Where buds have broken starry white.

Bowered in prunus blackest Puss
Set in snow branches crouching thus
Brings Night's small island home to us.

Two orange planets his eyes glow
Down at the spaniel's leaps below.
No stir will cat's sleek body show.

Like a colour print of calm Hiroshige
The scene's profound tranquillity
Foiled dog, blossom, the cat in the tree.

La Cathédrale Engloutie

(After Debussy)

Out of the misty tide the sailors see
Thrilled with sweet fear, the pale Cathedral rise
The pinnacled perfection! spectrally
Adorned with glistening spray to their wild eyes.

Sea fowl scream round the belfry and the bells
Desperate, salt-worn fierce jangle out of tune.
The structural vision sways; transience foretells
The solemn re-engulfing must come soon.

O poets, when from out your little day
Brief Beauty looms your hearts are stirred and won!
Creation sweetens all until the grey
Flat seas return and ecstasy is gone.

Fifty Summers Back

Fifty summers back
Bathing in elm shade
Sucking sorrel
I watched not boring cricket
But a booted conker-coloured horse
Dragging the shining roller.

Heard thunder
Above clanking
And click of bat on ball
Watched the envenomed sky
Heard wicked muffled guns from France.

Familiar behind a lightning lit chalk quarry
Beyond the North Downs
London lay, security, my home.
Mind failed to grasp

Quailed to sense
The uncouth agony of soldiers dying
Shot callously as random birds.

I had my own small violence
Sadistic bully
Precocious intimations of evil.

Both antechamber of crime
And kindly nurse
My prep school.

The House of Certainty

The house of certainty is roofless now
Cracked are the floors that taught me how to walk.
This was my brother's room. Tread soft, speak low
Lest voice wake echoes, fallen plaster talk.
Outside it is the same where windows gape
Like eyeless sockets blind which cannot see
The ravaged orchard blasted from its shape
The spate of torn leaves, blackened apple tree.
Only a furlong from the twisted shard
Of bomb beds of dark roses as before
Blossom in living pride: but O how hard
Such vibrant panache hits the heart still sore!
Murdered past days. Yet wondering praise I give
That though my home has died my loved ones live.

In Memoriam: Sidney Keyes

*(Killed in action, April 1943, within a
few weeks of his twenty-first birthday)*

Death stole his dreams and put away his treasure
Before his dreams were ripe, or we renewed,
Hurrying him into unfruitful limbo.
Tell me if Pity's head averted
Was ever sad like this?
The tree is down amidst a roar of leaves.
I mourn within the green glow of his thought.

O magnet war that drew this man to doom
Death that bereft him of his homecoming
Like Homer's demi-gods, what spite to us
The flexible and strong iambic roll
Broken, did you intend? The pity of it.
Stilled the big utterance, quiet the searching heart.

He was that buzzard, dying, which I saw
With eye yet eloquent, with the doomed eye.
He was a new tower springing like a lily,
Our fortress, yet with black guns trained upon it.
He was a cloister where soft doves were flying,
The voice of old and young and children crying.

His speech was silver as Demosthenes
His eye of observation like a knife.
For him all history hung upon a chain
Who made a rosary of the centuries
Telling the beads of Nature's lore and Time
Spanning the one and same.

Full is the mouth I watch, that gentleness
Speaking those deep-toned early poems of death.
He has died so young, so very young who has gone forward
Into the light we neither know nor guess.

Poem for Winter

I

In the closed season, ironbound days
When the clock is silent the heart ticks cold
Man chafes at failure void of praise.
By crystal paw sea's sweeping hair is held
The sea lies dead, no quick rage can rouse
Earth's old enemy too dumb to rave
Nothing of green comber, halcyon wave.
Yet in this time of hard salt and frozen tears
Fresh glory stirs beneath those white veneers.

When tilth is warmed by an eider quilt
While cornstacks shelter the powdered horse
Man fears the image of a hearse
Shrinks from ashes of evil his curious guilt
Raging at talent foolishly spilt;
By snow smooth roof, by duck-plumed holly
Envies the foraging bird, the long living tree.

II

In her stark season, stonebound hours
Woman half reads seeing a shadowed garden
Past curled hyacinths a bare calligraphy of boughs
Blue through her window. She would slough the burden
A serpent conscience harshly throws
At Life's lust. She knows the grave's not yet
She heeds more rending voices than regret
Hearing the loud worm knocking in the tree
Nebs of spring irised birds poking for pleasure
Exults that flames from darkness shall break free
As crafty stars pierce magicking earth's treasure.
Behind the dim frond bright flowers
Fountaining gold to greet love-enfolding hours.

III

In this dry day of rock seed-juices run
Through heart, leaf, root, their baffling chosen course.
Soul is man's weather so soon as blood's begun.
A dog's pink tongue drinks snow melted by sun;
Smudging the white field goes that yellow horse
Crushing blind crystals till they creek.
In woods' dark thickets yaffles lurk
Practising how to laugh their April joke.

Man in known misery of a wintry age
Divides his soul shunning the fecund earth
His matrix the mother; spurns in perplexed rage
Her patterned joy estranged from bliss of birth
Because one round proud swelling breast must pass
The sentence of the years on flesh and grass.

Punctually flows the solar tide of spring.
Timepiece the chiffchaff tick-tocks summer
Grey badger yells, brabbles the bunting
From August wires will wheeze the yellowhammer.
The nubile waves of Life shall quiver, break
Etheric cycle driven by a changing moon
The frore heart breathe to a hotter tune.
Faces of fear miss all a planet's wonder
Each maculation of this dust clot's splendour.

Saul At Endor

Saul the tall man, Saul the soldier, Saul the king
Grey hair dishevelled, his long beard untrim
Weeping, sought divination of a witch—
Coming through darkness to her dark bothy.

When the wise woman worked her barbarous charms
All she could show was matter for disaster,
The finger plucked from a Philistine corpse,
The Babylonian lore brought dreaded Samuel.

Cantankerous the face of that old man,
The fetch contorted from his livid hatred,
Arms, robes bright dripping with the blood of Agag
The hour the prophet hacked him limb from limb.

Sad was the soul of Saul, the Lord's Anointed
Because his mellow heart had taught him pity.
All lost, the underworld must black enfold him
Because the tree of ruth bore disobedience.

Saul the tall man, Saul the soldier, Saul the king
Loses tonight those brilliant eyes of heaven.
Tomorrow shatters the blue bowl of day
When Saul the soldier shall die in battle.

How Far Those Days of Peace Seem Now

How far those days of peace seem now:
The oast, the farmhouse, amber bees
Battling in wallflowers. Memory bestow
Lavender, lilies, the ecstasy
Which flowers and children brought you in past days!

How tranquil seem flown hours of peace:
Hop pickers by the barn, the damson tree.
That wealden pastoral bears for me
The impress of your soul, release.

One night of laughter, blessed with joys
We picked the damsons, looking through
The plum-black clusters, leaves to stars. For us
Life was discovered treasure, new.
A gold moon lit the orchard. With slow voice
You read the Idylls of Theocritus.

Life

1. PRAISE

A seed spirals.
Eggs are song.
Sunrise blesses
Day is long.

Babies strengthen
Limbs thrust
Gracing life
As limbs must.

2. LAMENT

A leaf shrivels
Thunder sighs,
Sunset splinters
Action dies.

Metals tarnish,
Moth, rust.
A bright eye
Dims to dust.

Lazarus

While Mary wept within her darkened room,
While Martha served the guests and broke her heart,
Where were you, Lazarus, those four days?
Not in the garden-tomb, cool from the sun
But in a world of light, glory beyond
The toys of sense, the fraud of Time.

'The undiscover'd country from whose bourn
No traveller returns'.—
But you, bewildered Lazarus, come back
Answering His mighty word of power:
'Lazarus, come forth!'
You stood, bound in your grave-clothes, in the sun
While awe fell on the shaking crowd,
Your amazed soul caged dumbly in your eye.

How could you, Lazarus, speak to them of that?
Words would fall baffled back
Beating against the doors of sense
The myth of Time.
How make the deaf to hear?
The blind to see?
So your soul kept a secret: unguessed Heaven.
Dazed, you walked softly all your length of hours
A silent man, a quiet man, remote
A man who guards a dream.

Poem for Autumn

(To John Trewin)

While faint-heart honeysuckle slackens her pale grip
Of rosegold claws in the tall untidy hedge
Where flashing flies, more torpid bees still tumble, sip;
While the slight river-chat slips restless through the sedge
Dark matron elms stand comfortably at peace;
Nor, solid to the heart, are English oaks
Mounds of brown gold: not yet will trees
Dressing for show, put on their gaudy cloaks;
Nor yet the lissom silver birch toss each bright curl
With the defiant gesture of a girl
Harried, but roused at being pursued, dancing
A brief ecstatic dance—with love advancing—
From her veins' ichor, the fugitive ballet Joy;
Before young blood has found her boy
Before youth's trophies have been won.
No poplar tempts as yet the westering miser sun
With fluttering of bright-minted million pennies.

Autumn comes in not suddenly with pomp
Of gold and purple flowers, with no loud trump,
But with an unexpected alien breath
Acid, like the taste of an apple on the lips;
Long before fruit mellows, stealthily creeps
With shadows, with a chill presage of death;
Much before huge Orion, old, so very old
Climbs up in staggering brilliance from the east;
Before the gaunt swift leaves for a fatter feast
Urged by black rapid scythe-shaped wings away
To find hot Egypt's sun another day,
His only enemy, here under faint skies, the cold.

Autumn approached last night, but quietly;
Laid skeins of gossamer, which light discloses,
Between bowing blooms; brought to the orchard tree
The blazoned wasps, that rich Red Admiral there
Fanning slow wings on a dropped rotting pear;
And pearled with rain the cold autumnal roses.

Out near the woods fading Rose Bay willowherb
Spills wool for seed; the sunbright fields disturb
With sight of fleece-scraps heavy sheep have left
In the cropped grass, that could be milky mushrooms.
Under the drip of trees in thickening glooms
By a mauve mallow clump, grow flat horse-mushrooms
As big as plates and nibbled, holed, the theft
Evidently of silent slug and snail.
The smoky sun begins to draw a veil
And one by one the thicker veils are cast
Down on the distant misty landscape half aghast
And hushed, till soon sly meshes of moonlight
Are tangled like pale scarves in oaks and elms.
The Tree of Night buds, all the branches bright
With stars for leaves. The silence overwhelms.
The heart of silence stirs, the fretted sky
Is charmed, arrested till a sudden cry
A white owl's shiver-note rings out the call to thought.

There is no sadness here, no death, but rest and resurrection.
See, how the tired leaves dream away their sleep!
Brown Autumn bears her own renewal and inverse perfection,
Brings certain promise and no mere rejection
Of life or hope, no crowded sorrow we should keep.
Though the dank aster hangs her head,
While Naked Ladies show no leaf,
Iron rust of sorrel pleads no cause for grief
Nor spent hard knapweed, for these are not dead.
While the cupped acorn holds the infant oak,
When ash-keyes hang, a colony of bats
Soon strongly rooted swelling midgets poke
Up through the soil, ubiquitous. Live beech-mast mats
The forest floor, while nature turns another page
Of tender primrose leaves in the year's circling pilgrimage.

The solar Word, the seed are over all:
Behold a glory great! where light and earth
Between them shall accomplish each new birth,
Of myriad miracles be prodigal;
Etheric bodies building up from sun and soil such flowers
To glow with complex beauty transient hours.
So seed-grain burns like a small nubilous cloud

With visible magic luminously endowed;
As when a dog fox trotting through the dark
Pursues his lady with compelling bark
And the roused vixen hears his frenzied yelp,
Feels first the instance of her unborn whelp;
As when the egg lurks in the song of lark:
Thus Nature keeps her pause, unfolds her plan
To mould a plant, a fox, a lark, or man.

This is the height, the time when trees and shrubs are flaring
With tawny gipsy scarves, all colour-trumpets blaring
Bronze, blood, and brassy notes, the tulip tree's high yellow,
The sumach's purple plush, vermilion berries, with a hundred
    tints, some savage, mellow
Black, umber, buff, scarlet and gold, metallic green, a challenge
    proudly pleasant
As Phasian firebird, the cock archly-stepping pheasant;
Before quiet Winter brings his cold device
The time Jack pike lies rigid under ice—
Of crystal branches humming to numbed ears
When trees can tinkle like old chandeliers.

Now drops the withered day, the twilight droops, the Milky Way
Glimmers a broad cherishing silver stream across the sky.
How lightly step the Twins in Gemini
Dancing to the celestial choreography!
Valiant Orion strides forth, protects from harm
With flaming of his golden sword the farm,
Flashing above oasts round and warm . . .

Let us acquiesce.

Butterflies, Moths

Not till earth's flowers bloomed came butterflies
And moths and bees, to probe their nectaries.

I grew from childhood mad on butterflies
To boyhood's wonder, evidence of eyes;
Opening a drawer to see my latest prize
Pinned firm and neatly set
In its white cabinet.

The hunt was all: an aerial flower
The Swallow-tail would span an hour
Some foreign grove, floating
Skimming, rising, falling—my eyes gloating;
Or a flight of Clouded Yellows passing over,
Tarrying, breeding on the Cornish clover.
Or, flitting by on Orange-tippèd wing
Past hedge cow-parsley of an English spring,
A deepening joy, as certain harbinger
As cuckoo ever was of summer near.

Once more a burnished metal chrysalis
Has cracked its chitin; I would yield for this
Many an hour of more abitious bliss
Watching the fresh imago dry close by,
A Greenish Silver-washed Fritillary
Lucent with new-found life on a thistle head,
Fanning wide wings, framed in the forest glade.
O! there I go with bag of tarletan
Talk to the woodman, hunting where I can.

Not till earth's flowers came fell butterflies
A damascened florescence from the skies.

I see Buddleia in exultant bloom:
Fat mauve thick-scented spears against an arch
Of burning Dog Day blue, (hearing the zoom
Of loading bees and iridescent flies)

Mustering scarlet bands and Peacock eyes;
Small Tortoiseshells, bright 'soldier butterfly'
For soldiers once wore red; now come and go
A Speckled Wood, and Garden Whites and Blues,
A Small Copper's penetrating glow,
A Painted Lady's orange-tawny hues.

Here near the sandhills' gold the ragwort blows
Where colonies, ringed yellow-black, expose
On crowded plants ill-tasting warning colour,
The larvae of the pretty Cinnabar
A flyer weak at evening. Dashes past
A male Oak Eggar on voluptuous quest;
Sex, borne for many miles upon the weather
From nubile female torpid in the heather.

As light departs, with autumn starlight shed
Mildly in woodland it is time to spread
The treacle-trap upon rough bark of trees
Of sugar brown, rum, syrup and the lees
Of hops compounded, so the moths may drink
That soon to half-drunk lethargy will sink.

I light a shuttered lantern; make the round,
Pill-box the different prizes to be found
Those owl-faced moths that nod with fiery eye
Wings still, raised high, or dithering frenziedly.

If Lepidoptera's English names mean poetry
I name only a fraction to recall
Those hours of venture, exaltation; scrawl
At random what was poetry to me:
Adonis Blue, The Queen of Spain Fritillary,
Old Lady, Peach Blossom and Kentish Glory,
The Crimson Speckled Footman, Burnished Brass,
Green Silver Lines, Large Emerald, Red Sword-grass;
Piratical, prodigious the Death's Head,
Swift, Magpie, ghostly Leopard at a light.
Enough. They pass, wonders of day and night.

The drawers return. The key is turned once more.
And now embalmed within this written score
Before black mites powder such charms of earth,
Symbols which childhood's dreaming brought to birth.
Psyche the Greeks called butterflies—the soul.

The need to kill no longer makes my goal
But to preserve each living thing from ill.
No blood of creature would I spill.

Rather, I'd watch and joy to see
Life-holy excellence of what may be.
Such patterned tapestries in motion, sense
Flying with varied range of eloquence.

The Butterfly

(To Julia)

I caught a Swallow-tail inside my hat
To send you in a letter, redolent
Of sun and savage mountains, blossom too
Lush grass and teeming flowers, bringing you
The Alpine breath.
                But when I picked him out
He glowed so fiercely, not a feather dimmed,
His six legs waving protest, could I kill him?
Brilliant his blue eye-spots; his wings were saffron.
It would have been a blasphemy against Day.
He was Life-holy. So I let him soar
Up, if he wished, to meet the glinting glacier.
He must shine, if he will, upon my page.

Oleander

Oleander bush,
from lean dark buds
a fountain of rose.

Suddenly in southern sun
a firespray of pink sparks,
a floral jet
flushing the polished sky.

Oleander moth
nature's nonpareil.

Archetype
of Vinci's dream,
a lumbering
soaring
scythe-winged
plump, pointed
owl-faced aeroplane,
with thread-fine antennae.

Oleander Hawk
paragon
of insect wonder.

Hawk-moth
smooth velvet
olive brown green-marbled beauty!

Itea, Gulf of Corinth.

Greek Folk Song

*(The olives on Corfu are small and brown.
The peasants sometimes call a mole on the
body an 'olive')*

Goats to raise, goats to graze,
Drawing of water, daily the milking,
The endless olives to pick.

So went my love
With her head kerchiefed, in thick clothes
Working all day, too busy to smile.

But at night when the sun went down
She was not busy.

There was an olive on her brown arm
And her breasts were like lemons
And her thighs were lithe in love as fishes.

The Theophilos Museum, Mytilene

'Theophilus gave us a new eye.'—*George Seferis*

(Theophilos Hadjimichael (1873–1934) a primitive folk artist of original genius much of whose work, now internationally accepted, is exhibited in the Theophilos Museum at Varia, Mytilene.)

In this small house that holds
    Courage, a painter's eye,
The Greek hillside enfolds
    a timeless treasury.

The vision Theophilos gave
    with his volition grew.
The past, his joy to save
    more than he ever knew.

Compulsion of a child
    to mix his colours right.
Detached, a nature mild
    expressed each new delight.

Here on half-holiday
    Greek schoolgirls lighten love;
Loll, talk or simply play
    threading the almond grove

with star-flowers in brushed hair,
    Dresses blue as blue sea,
laugh, run through the olives there.
    Then one throws echoingly

a ball straight to her friend,
    As a king's daughter once
on the Phaeacian sand
    Played out her deathless game.

From Ormos Grikou, Patmos

Make your own Eden, since Edens are lost in the world's
  embrace.

A flotilla of noisy ducks pass by
Like ships of the line.

Build your own castles, though men's castles are built on sand;
(Yellow birds shift and fidget in the chiaroscuro of a tamarisk)
Drawbridges are useless planks.

Take refuge in Hellas or Byzantium
Though here between shore and a humped volcanic islet
No winedark sea, no laughter-loving Aphrodite
Rises from shot-green argent.

The fortress Monastery on its high hill
Repeats John's calm assurance of God's Love,
While I hear the harsh cock-crow that overthrew Peter.

From Taormina Once

Do you remember how once from Taormina
In the noon's heat we chose a mule plod
Up to Mola; the path coiled like a serpent
Round the mountainside, past prickly pear and olives?
And as we zig-zagged, toiled in steep ascent
We saw Etna smoking tirelessly,
Her brilliant snowline cut out on the blue
With one snail-track of lava, almost new
Crawling towards a smeared white-feathered sea.

Have you forgotten those terraced vines and cornlands
Which at first draped the enormous rocks? And finally
When we had passed beyond Mola, looking back
On flat red roofs below us; at such a height Etna seemed
Higher, taller—to have climbed, too, with us!

Clearly I can recall sounds: bells, roosters, donkeys.
But most I remember the rest we made long
On the way down; honeysweet wild love, avid as Eros.
At length I took a book from my pocket,
Calverley's *Theocritus*, to read your favourite idyll.
Remember how a goatherd then came by
With his flock of white goats, after fresh grazing?
And nothing changed for twenty centuries!
By will of Providence, or chance, the boy stopped
Near us, mouth open, black eyes absurdly lit
Startled to hear a Syracusan song
In words he could not understand.
He was—must have been—called Corydon or Delphis!
He stayed. We stayed. You smiled. I read again:
'*Bethink thee, mistress Moon, whence came my love.*'

Abroad

My need to capture Nature,
Each fleeting feature—
Sights, sounds, scents, texture and taste.
The call comes back, returns compulsively.
Much runs to waste.

I watch a villa courtyard hard to indite,
Rose walls, green shutters, seeing sharply
What divisions of light and shade
On half-circle steps the sun has made.
A black cat breathes in the shade.

Look! there's the least movement of a white poplar's
Small honey-silk leaves. The cypress moves a dark tip.

When from Avignon I shall slip homeward gratefully
Am gone,
I will remember carefully tended dry soil
Blossom, the fruits of toil
And unsparing light on the broad quick flow of the Rhône.

Each Quiddity

In Life each creature's quiddity
Is not skin-deep, but God's beauty
Integral to each living thing
Which flower and bird and mammal bring.

Remove a woman's cloud of hair
No longer is that woman there.
Dock a squirrel's flambeau tail
Arborial leaping then must fail,
Appropriate to a grounded rat.
Seal-points sign a Siamese cat.

Where black sea raves flung spume illumes
With rainbow lightness; calm assumes.
Lichens cling tight on roofs, round rocks.
Seas wax and wane in tidal shocks.

Seven snake-necked swans, a Murex spire
Motion, stillness each require.
Both may equally strike fire!
Inbeings of earth's variorum
Violent turmoil, a shell's decorum.

To Candida Born

Child, star-born under rays we little know—
Forces which through the void of long lost silent aeons go—
From what Creative Heart come you our way
With beautiful strength of weakness, so potent in least play?

Have you life knowledge of sainthood or of sin?
While you lie limber in cot, move limbs like frond or fin,
Such powerful daintiness intangibly
Moves firm as tides that draw the rhythmic moon-bound sea.

At the alpha is touch: teach questing lips!—
Dark to what lifts, affrights—no portent of rage, sweet soul's eclipse;
No towering tongues of fire, no rapture. None other
Charms today but warmth, this grace, the softened shadow of your mother.

How soon will brightest candour of your eyes
Set seal upon your name, flashing a lustrous white disguise,
Blinding what's ugly, poor pennants of blackness furled;
While your wisdom-look throws us signals from another world.

Comfort

Through icicles the morning sun has made
A Christmas-tree illusion; beauty false
As glittering gold, a savage debt unpaid
To reason, as romantic as a waltz!
For I confused such brightness with the spring
With singing birds and flowers. Earth showed her mettle.
With dawn the new-turned soil did surely bring
A glow like light pours on a copper kettle.
Oh, never say that spring can come too soon,
For May means friends' kindnesses, mellow chat.
And loneliness is evil. Summer's boon
Will heal my complexes; blest more than that
   Will bring her joy who in her life-long part
   Has held, and holds, the essence of my heart.

In Time Of Tribulation

I

In timeless childhood green grew day
As Eden, when I rushed to play

With lightfoot feet: a butterfly
An Angel then, not doomed to die.

Happy, I gave a loving pledge
To crimson-berried hawthorn hedge

To honeysuckle's rose-gold claws
To seagull, nuthatch, finches, daws.

And to each season's colour. Spring
No more than Winter seemed to sing!

The whole world sang. But sometimes night
With terror presaged future plight

Precocious thoughts of evil pressed,
Alarming rapture, killing rest.

With lambent limbs and flowing hair
Girls came and trod a golden stair

So that I saw them queenly. More,
Gave Helen's name to a plain whore.

But soon to crumble breast, throat, groin;
Lust gives exchange in its own coin

And unloved girls are fleeting. No,
I found I would not have it so.

II

But holy Love made all things sweet.
We knew not what fresh joys to greet,

The plainest teacup in your hand
Brought pleasures we had never planned,

The night sky budding into stars
Orion and the dark red Mars.

Great things and small things. Best of all
The silence in a waterfall.

Silence is best, for then the soul
Goes searching how to plumb the whole

Cosmos, the wonder, mystery, pain,
A mite of God's vast wealth to gain.

And God's in all, in mountains, sea:
Each creature in its quiddity.

In curled cat, in twining snake
The owl blinking to keep awake

The sagging tiger, slow-coach snail
The armadillo, lace-wing frail.

And so my verse will never greet
Charades of shame, Coursing, the Meet.

II

The party's over. The play is done.
The curtain falls on a dead sun.

Old friends drop out and Time must end,
Life's gaudies pass for foe and friend,

Alone I fear to front cold sky
Alone I face Eternity.

IV

Christ said, when you have run the race
'For you I go prepare a place'.

He surely could have told us more?
The foolish try to jump the score

In séances, the medium's spell.
What lies beyond we cannot tell.

Yet to the man who deeply prays
'All shall be well' Dame Julian says.

V

Today I've seen my country grow
From great to small, from high to low

And honour broken, the lean kine
The Word unspoken, diluted wine.

But while a warbler-Ariel still
Preserves my freedom's flight from ill,

So shall I try to cast my care
In knowledge the Almighty's there.

When the World ends God will decide.
Man in God's ruling must abide.

If man destroys himself, so be it.
No bomb can kill the crystal spirit.

Two Silences

1. SNOWFLAKES

Black snowflakes crowd thickening
Swirling from a sepia sky
Lightly rocking gondalas,
Silent touch grass-blades.

Goosefeather snow
Flakes hexagonal
None identical
Unique as a voice
Limitless as finger-prints.

2. THE CHURCHYARD

The churchyard under the moon, quiet as glass,
Shows like a host of Moslems crouched in prayer.

Be Still Then . . .

(Psalm 46: 10)

Be still then, and know that I am God.
Recall moments—remember Darien—
How Love was born, words unspoken
Or whispers a token
Of sight, touch,
The dumb how much?

Noise destroys.
Deafened, I hear nothing.

Majestic clouds, shadows on the grass
Tell how a summer evening passed.
Stilled all din of loathing
I listen to the silent lips of peace
Birds' rest, flowers' hush, human release.

Evensong

Pink sky at evening
Cattle on grass
Shadows;
Short days of winter
Pass.

Each day a bonus
Allowed to me
Now crisp hours dwindle
Hurriedly.

Each winter morning
The sun lifts his eye:
Such beauties will prosper
After I die.

May I have power to sing
More truthful song
Before to a greater largeness
I belong.